AFTER A BREAKUP

A book for women

(Revised Version)

INOSIA GEORGES (M)

Copyright © 2024 Inosia Georges

All rights reserved

CONTENTS

Acknowledgements 5

Preface 9

Introduction 11

Chapter 1: *Breaking Up* 16

Chapter 2: *Reacting To A Break-Up –*

"Ahh Well, His Loss!" 36

Chapter 3: *Keeping A Low Profile* 52

Chapter 4: *Hobby Time* 64

Chapter 5: *TRAVEL. FULL. STOP*   80

Chapter 6: *Become A Boss*   102

Chapter 7: *Set Goals And Win*   118

Chapter 8: *A Survey about why Men Leave*   38

Chapter 9: *Talking To New People*   145

Chapter 10: *Always Put God First*   160

Conclusion: *Recovery And Moving On*   169

Guides and References   173

About the Author   187

ACKNOWLEDGEMENTS

This book is dedicated to my mother, Isnara Georges, whose unwavering faith and powerful prayers have been the cornerstone of my journey. Mom, your prayers have been a guiding light, and your strength has taught me the true meaning of waiting on God. Your wisdom and support have been my pillar through the toughest times, and I can't thank you enough for guiding me away from the path of revenge and towards healing and growth.

I also want to give a special shoutout to Melan—just had to throw that in! I am blessed to have a sister like you who fights for me — thank you for always standing by my side. Your encouragement and love have been crucial in this journey, and I am forever grateful.

To Semaj O. R. Seymour and Neteca Smith, your financial support provided me with the stability I needed to focus and finish this book. Your generosity has paved the way for me to think clearly and bring this work to life.

To my late pastor, Bishop Rodney J. Roberts, who tirelessly worked to instill godly principles in us all. His dedication to guiding us through the toughest times and his efforts to help mend my relationship and ease my heartache were invaluable. His wisdom and care have left a lasting impact on my life.

To Prophet Silvan Farquharson and Apostle Areitha Jones, your foresight and blessings have been a source of strength throughout the creation of this book. Your support and encouragement have paved the way for many more works to come. Thank you for believing in this journey from the start.

To my father, God, my eternal strength and guiding light. I was lost at times, yet you never let me fail. In moments when I felt abandoned or thought you didn't care, you performed miracles that reminded me of your unwavering presence. Your guidance has been the cornerstone of my life, teaching me the power of surrender and trust.

Heartache is a painful chapter I hope never to revisit, but through your teachings, I have learned the power of letting go and allowing you to take control.

Thank you all for being a part of this journey and for your divine influence in my life.

PREFACE

Most people who have been through a bad break-up have a story to tell. Each experience is unique, and sometimes the pain can feel so overwhelming that it seems no one else could possibly understand. But remember, you are not alone.

I wrote this book to guide you towards healing, sparing you from unnecessary suffering and the desire for revenge. Within these pages, you'll find moments that are hilarious, insightful, and engaging. I encourage you to let go of the fear of the unknown and to explore the suggestions with an open heart. Embrace the journey and discover how laughter and new perspectives can lead to profound healing.

As you read through these chapters, take a moment to clear your mind and approach the content with an open heart. By the end of this book, I'm confident you'll find yourself smiling. I can promise you that much.

INTRODUCTION

Ending a relationship is never easy. When the human heart falls in love, it binds deeply to another, merging spirits in a profound connection. Break-ups, therefore, can be incredibly painful. This book is for anyone—whether you're contemplating a break-up, experiencing one, or have recently ended a relationship. You don't have to fear what's unfolding. By taking a moment to relax and reflect on your situation, you'll find clarity and direction. Remember, this isn't the end of your story—it's a new beginning.

As someone who faced a sudden break-up after a long marriage, I understand the searing pain of discovering betrayal from someone I thought loved me. During this time, I came to some important realizations.

Firstly, my ex wasn't sharing my pain; he was out living their life while I was left to struggle at home. The chapters ahead will explore in-depth strategies to give yourself the break you deserve and to shift the focus away from your ex. It won't be easy, and you'll need to decide if you're ready to seek help. But know this: you have the power to transform your experience and find healing.

Once you decide to move on, the steps to healing will become much clearer. With time, you'll look back and find yourself able to laugh at the things that once seemed so overwhelming.

To handle break-ups effectively, it's crucial to understand one key principle: people change. This book will guide you through why it's important not to rush into new relationships immediately. Further chapters will provide more insights into navigating this initial stage and offer practical advice for moving forward.

Secondly, it's important to recognize that anger won't resolve your situation. Avoid letting anger take over after a disagreement or break-up.

The tips and insights shared in this book come from my personal experiences as well as the stories of others I've encountered. If you find yourself disagreeing with any part, take a moment to reflect, then move forward. Remember, no one expects you to get over your ex immediately. However, dwelling on thoughts and memories for too long can hinder your ability to heal and move on.

For now, focus on reading and absorbing the ideas that resonate with you or make you smile. As you begin to heal, you may find yourself drawn to explore the deeper meaning and purpose behind this book. Enjoy the journey!

CHAPTER 1
BREAKING UP

At the beginning of a relationship, we rarely foresee that it might end in discord and break-up. It's natural to fall for someone who treats you well, so don't blame yourself if you find yourself in this situation.

It's not always easy to recognize when a relationship is faltering. Often, we wish we could communicate our issues more effectively, find clear answers, resolve conflicts, and move forward. But sometimes, things don't unfold as we had hoped or planned.

In many situations, when women detect something shady or suspicious, it's common to react with frustration. We often jump to conclusions, confront the man, and pass judgment based on our suspicions. Our initial reaction might be to question his whereabouts or actions, assuming our version of events is the only truth. This instinct to investigate and seek answers is natural, but it's crucial to approach these situations with a mindset geared towards understanding rather than condemnation.

On the other hand, there are relationships where a woman might sense something is off but feels hesitant to ask questions, fearing that doing so might spark an argument. This hesitation can stem from a variety of concerns, such as the potential for conflict or a lack of confidence in how the question will be received. However, it's important to remember that avoiding difficult conversations often doesn't solve the underlying issue and can lead to greater misunderstandings.

In any relationship, fostering an environment where both partners feel safe to express their concerns and ask questions without fear of conflict is vital. Open communication is the foundation of trust and understanding. If there's a recurring pattern of avoiding tough conversations, it may be beneficial to address why that fear exists and work together to create a more transparent and supportive dialogue.

At the beginning of most relationships, everything feels exciting and respectful, often driven by initial attraction and lust. However, understanding why break-ups happen requires a deeper look into how relationships evolve.

First, consider why you entered the relationship in the first place. If you've expressed that you're only looking for fun, it's crucial to recognize that this often sets the stage for a more superficial connection. Even if you transition to a committed relationship, be aware that dynamics can shift. People sometimes change after reaching certain milestones, such as becoming intimate, or as the relationship's vibe transforms.

To build a lasting and meaningful connection, it's important to approach dating with patience. Resist the urge to rush into deep emotions. Instead, take the time to truly get to know the other person. By pacing yourself, you create a stronger foundation and avoid the pitfalls of falling too quickly. This deliberate approach can help you establish a relationship built on genuine understanding and respect, rather than fleeting attraction.

This is the perfect moment to ask questions, set clear boundaries, and establish your standards. I always advise my sisters to let the new boyfriend or date take the lead in expressing his interest through actions. If he wants to cover expenses on a date or give you gifts, let him do so graciously. Embrace these gestures without hesitation, as if you are accustomed to being treated well.

Should the relationship end, you won't have to look back with regret or feel that your time was wasted. Accepting gifts and surprises is perfectly acceptable—don't feel the need to return them or reject his gestures. By allowing him to express his interest in the way he chooses, you ensure that your standards are communicated clearly from the start. This way, you minimize potential conflicts later on.

Remember, by accepting these gestures, you are not obligating yourself to reciprocate beyond your comfort level. Consider them as a form of acknowledgment for the time you've spent together. This approach helps you maintain your self-respect and ensures that you enter and exit relationships with clarity and confidence.

Fights

Arguments and fights are a natural part of any relationship, often arising when both partners feel strongly about an issue. However, responding with anger or withdrawing into silence rarely helps resolve the situation or benefit your mental well-being. Some men might let you stew in your frustration, while others might ignore your silence, especially if you're in the wrong. It's crucial not to jump to conclusions or make assumptions based on these reactions.

Sometimes, conflicts stem from attempts to uncover information in a way that might be perceived as confrontational. From your perspective, it might seem like a straightforward question that deserves an answer. Yet, the response can often be defensive or evasive, leaving you frustrated. Some men, adept at navigating tricky situations, may even shift the focus and accuse you of something else, changing the subject entirely.

In these situations, it's essential to approach conflicts with a clear mind and avoid letting emotions dictate your responses. Open, honest communication is key. Instead of escalating tensions, try to understand the underlying issues and address them constructively. This approach helps in navigating arguments more effectively and maintaining a healthier dynamic in the relationship.

As women, it's important to be both perceptive and assertive in our relationships. If a man accuses you of causing problems by asking questions or digging into an issue, it's okay to acknowledge that your intention is to address the problem. This reaction might make him defensive, which could suggest he's hiding something or feeling cornered. It's a natural response, but it often complicates the situation further.

When you start expressing your concerns and speculating about what might be happening, it's easy for the conversation to escalate into arguments. This can lead to revisiting past issues and grievances, which only adds to the emotional strain. If he responds by ignoring your concerns or becoming dismissive, it can make you feel even more frustrated.

In these moments, try to approach the situation with empathy and patience. Focus on addressing the immediate issue without letting past conflicts overshadow the conversation. Open, honest communication, paired with a calm demeanor, can help resolve misunderstandings and build a stronger, more understanding relationship. By staying grounded and compassionate, you can navigate these challenges more effectively and maintain a healthier dynamic.

The Truce break-up

I refer to this concept as "the peace treaty" between partners. It's when both individuals reach a mature understanding that the relationship isn't evolving as they had hoped and agree to part ways amicably. Contrary to what some might think, these kinds of breakups are becoming more common. There are various reasons why couples decide to end their relationship together.

Some people may prefer to avoid unnecessary drama and choose to part ways peacefully. Others might find themselves too busy with their careers or personal goals to invest the time and energy required to sustain the relationship. In some cases, couples who frequently break up and reconcile may eventually reach a point where they feel there's no more emotional energy left to save the relationship, even if one person still holds feelings of love.

For many, especially those focused on their careers and personal success, the choice to move on without conflict is a pragmatic one. They prioritize their paths and goals over the complexities of the relationship, opting for a respectful and peaceful separation. This approach allows both partners to move forward without unnecessary drama, understanding that their paths are diverging in a way that respects their individual needs and aspirations.

The silent break-up

Some people choose to end things abruptly, going "cold turkey." This means they suddenly cut off all communication, stopping texts and calls entirely after deciding to end the relationship. It can be quite jarring when someone you were interested in just disappears without a word.

Have you ever had that moment when, despite initial excitement, your interest in someone just fades away? I know I have. It's surprising how quickly feelings can shift from the first date to the weeks that follow. This is a tough reality of modern dating, but it's something many of us encounter.

In these situations, I find it effective to block and delete their number from my phone. Let me explain why this approach makes sense. Often, especially with those who are more self-centered, once they've decided they're no longer interested, they'll simply cut off communication. They prioritize their own needs and move on without giving you any closure or explanation.

By taking the step to remove their contact details, you're not just avoiding the frustration of dealing with someone who has already made their disinterest clear. You're also protecting your own emotional well-being and taking control of your dating experience. It's a proactive way to move forward with dignity and focus on connections that truly matter to you.

It's all too common to find yourself in a situation where someone leads you to believe you're in a relationship, only to disappear suddenly after things become intimate. This can leave you feeling confused, guilty, and questioning yourself or wondering if there's someone else involved.

If you find yourself in this situation, here's what you need to do: block and delete him. Understand that he's just lost the best part of his life, and you deserve far better than to be left with unanswered questions and lingering doubts. Don't waste your time trying to chase him down, send apologies, or seek explanations.

Some men will end a relationship abruptly, without any goodbyes or explanations. In such cases, the best approach is to close that chapter and move forward as if it never happened. Prioritize your own happiness and well-being. You don't need to invest time and energy in someone who isn't willing to offer you the respect and clarity you deserve.

Regardless of the nature of the breakup, it's undeniable that all breakups bring pain. The first crucial step in moving on is determining whether you're truly finished or if you want to try again. Remember, the outcome often depends on how we choose to respond to these situations.

In the next chapter, we'll explore strategies for navigating breakups and responding in ways that might surprise others—and yourself. By focusing on how you handle these challenges, you'll see a significant improvement in your mood and attitude. Get ready to build the resilience you need to move on and thrive. See you in the next chapter!

As you navigate through the end of a relationship, it's important to ask yourself some key questions to guide your path forward:

- **Where do you see yourself five years from now?**

  Reflect on your long-term goals and aspirations. Are they aligned with the person you were with, or do you envision a different future for yourself?

- **Did you receive the support you needed from your partner?**

  Consider whether the relationship contributed positively to your personal growth and well-being. Was there mutual support and encouragement, or did you often feel unsupported?

- **Is getting back with this person right now a good idea?**

Evaluate the current situation honestly. Are the issues that led to the breakup resolved, or are they likely to resurface? Think about whether rekindling the relationship would genuinely benefit your future or simply repeat past patterns.

These reflections will help you assess whether reconnecting is truly in your best interest. Moving forward thoughtfully and focusing on your own growth and happiness will guide you toward a more fulfilling path.

CHAPTER 2

REACTING TO A BREAK-UP – "AHH WELL, HIS LOSS!"

When someone has made up their mind to leave, what can you really do? It's time for women to embrace a mindset of indifference. Ask yourself: what makes him believe that leaving is better for him and not for you? Don't let any man make you feel like he holds the power to determine your happiness.

If a man tells you he wants to end the relationship and pursue other people, don't hesitate—show him the door! Even if you need to put on a brave face, stand firm and act as though you were contemplating the same thing.

In the aftermath of a fight and separation, if he doesn't reach out, don't take on the role of the 'negotiator.' Resist the urge to text or call first, no matter how much it burns inside you. Trust me on this: holding back will empower you and help you move forward with strength and dignity.

Men often have a lot of pride, and believe it or not, he might actually be expecting you to make the first move. Some men assume that women are weaker and more likely to chase after them, but it's crucial not to fall into that trap. Even if it feels challenging, resist the urge to call him first.

After a breakup, it's natural for both parties to become distant and want solitude. This time alone often leads to replaying events and trying to pinpoint what went wrong. For many women, the impulse to call and apologize can be strong, but resist that urge. Why apologize for something you didn't do wrong? It's important to remember that it takes two to have a conflict, and even if you initiated the argument, it doesn't mean you're solely at fault.

Instead of dwelling on the past, focus on occupying your mind and moving forward.

Here are some constructive ways to keep yourself from overthinking:

- **Engage in New Hobbies:** Find activities that excite you and keep you occupied.

- **Focus on Personal Goals:** Channel your energy into achieving personal or professional milestones.

- **Connect with Friends and Family:** Spend time with those who uplift and support you.

- **Practice Self-Care:** Prioritize activities that enhance your well-being and happiness.

By staying active and focusing on your own growth, you'll find it easier to move on and embrace a brighter future.

First and foremost, surround yourself with positive, uplifting people who focus on anything but your ex. Avoid those who pry too much about what happened; instead, seek out friends who will engage with you on topics that bring you joy and distraction.

If you feel the need to vent, find a special friend who can listen without judgment. It's crucial to have someone who understands that venting is a necessary part of the healing process. These friends can provide a safe space for you to express your frustrations and emotions.

While it's natural for friends to have their own lives and commitments, cherish the time you have with them. Embrace their presence and allow yourself to fully enjoy their company.

One of the toughest times can be late at night, when thoughts of your ex can become overwhelming and tempting you to reach out. To manage these moments, I used to find places to go or activities to engage in until late. Keeping busy helps to avoid those vulnerable times when you're most likely to pick up the phone.

By surrounding yourself with positivity and staying active, you can navigate the aftermath of a breakup more effectively and create a path toward healing and renewal.

To keep your mind occupied and to prepare yourself for a restful night's sleep, find activities that engage and exhaust you. I remember spending time at a salsa club downtown where I felt a vibrant connection with the Latino community and immersed myself in a lively atmosphere. It was my way of meeting new people and expanding my horizons. While your activity might not be salsa dancing, the idea is to find something that energizes you and shifts your focus away from the breakup. When I first wrote this book, I hadn't yet fully grasped the profound power of the word of God. For those who are open to exploring faith, consider seeking Jesus and allowing His guidance to lead you towards what truly matters. Embracing spiritual wisdom can be a transformative influence, contributing significantly to your personal growth and future development. Let

His guidance help you navigate life's challenges with renewed strength and purpose.

So, make a decisive choice: either let go completely or revisit the drama. If you choose to move on, do it with style and confidence. Don't waste time at home crying—trust me, your ex is out there living his life and might even be seeing someone new.

This book is not about him; it's all about you. The key to moving on is understanding that tears won't solve relationship issues. It's time to be strong and take action. Get up, dress up, and show up with a renewed sense of self. Revamp your look with a fresh hairstyle, vibrant lipstick, and a new wardrobe if you can. You are beautiful, and you still have so much to offer. Embrace this attitude and let it fuel your journey to a better you.

It's important to keep a clear and compelling reason in mind for why the breakup was the right choice. For instance, I used to remind myself that I didn't want to be with someone who was unfaithful and slept around with random women. Whenever the temptation to reconcile arose, I would reflect on the negative consequences of his actions—the potential risks and the emotional damage. This helped me stay focused and grateful for the end of a harmful relationship.

I encourage you to think of something significant that he did that was not cool. This isn't about holding onto resentment, but rather about using your memories to keep away.

Forgiveness is important, but it doesn't mean you need to return to a relationship that was damaging. Keep these memories as a reminder of why you made the right choice. When feelings of weakness or doubt arise, and you're tempted to reach out, let these reflections strengthen your resolve and remind you why moving on was the best decision for your well-being.

Why are you checking up on him?

Whenever you feel the urge to check up on your ex, ask yourself this crucial question: Does he check up on me? Now answer.

It's common for women to struggle with the impulse to text or call their ex after a breakup, especially if there's a desire to salvage the relationship. However, reaching out when he has explicitly asked for space is rarely a good idea and can often push him further away. In fact, if he senses you're going to contact him, he might preemptively block you, especially if he perceives you as being emotional or desperate.

Men and women handle breakups differently. While many women may react emotionally, refuse to eat, or obsess over their ex, men are often less inclined to display similar behaviors unless they are still invested. It's important to recognize that, while you may feel overwhelmed and tempted to reach out, maintaining your dignity and self-respect is crucial.

Remember, refusing to eat or neglecting your well-being only weakens you. You need your strength, both physically and emotionally, to navigate this challenging time. Focus on nurturing yourself and building resilience. Your energy is better spent on self-care and personal growth rather than on trying to reconnect with someone who has chosen to step away.

More often than not, your ex isn't worth sacrificing your well-being over. Instead of letting the breakup consume you, keep yourself busy and focused on your own life. Let him wonder why you haven't reached out or tried to reconnect. His curiosity about whether you still care will lead him to reflect on his own actions and possibly even reach out to check on you.

Use this time to stay composed and allow things to unfold naturally. As you focus on yourself and clear your mind, you'll start to uncover new insights and strengths you never knew you had. This period of self-discovery can be incredibly enlightening and empowering.

Ask yourself: What are the things you've discovered about yourself during this time that you hadn't realized before? Embracing these revelations can help you move forward with confidence and clarity.

Write your thoughts here

_____

_____

_____

_____

_____

_____

What are some reasons why you SHOULD NOT call/go back/see him?

_____

_____

_____

_____

_____

_____

Chapter 3

Keeping a Low Profile

This chapter explores the power of maintaining a low profile and keeping your movements private for a while. It's crucial to be discerning about who you confide in, as not everyone in your circle may have your best interests at heart. Remember, every friend has their own network, and before you know it, your personal matters could be shared far beyond your control.

To effectively keep a low profile, start by limiting your social media activity. One of the most puzzling things for someone who is curious about you is not being able to track your updates online. When you stop sharing your whereabouts and personal details, it can spark their curiosity, leading them to dig deeper through social media or mutual acquaintances to piece together what's going on in your life.

By taking these steps, you not only protect your privacy but also give yourself the space and time needed to heal and move forward without unnecessary distractions or intrusions.

For now, it's essential to keep your personal affairs private. Allow people to remain in the dark about your progress and transformation following a breakup. By maintaining a low profile, you're giving yourself the space to evolve into the person you aspire to be. This period of privacy helps you witness your own growth and understand the benefits of stepping away from the past.

Additionally, limit the number of people you confide in. I recommend trying this approach for a week and observing its impact. Focus on distancing yourself from negative friends and family members who may not be sensitive to your emotions at this time. Instead, surround yourself with supportive individuals who listen and offer genuine companionship.

It's also crucial to seek guidance and discernment from God during this period. Turn to Him for wisdom and clarity as you navigate through your emotions and decisions. Prayer and reflection can provide you with a deeper understanding of your purpose and direction, helping you to stay grounded and focused.

In moments of uncertainty, ask for divine insight to discern what is best for your future. Trust that God's guidance will lead you towards opportunities that align with your true self and help you make choices that foster growth and healing.

Incorporate spiritual practices into your daily routine, such as prayer or reading the bible, to strengthen your faith and find peace amidst the changes. By aligning yourself with God's guidance, you can gain the inner strength and reassurance needed to move forward with confidence and resilience.

Also, every day take the time to dress up and capture photos of yourself. Recognize and appreciate your beauty and strength, especially when you smile. Keep these photos in your gallery as a reminder of your resilience and self-worth but hold off on posting them for now. This practice not only boosts your self-esteem but also reinforces your commitment to personal growth.

Taking a break from social media can significantly reduce the stress of worrying about others' opinions. However, if you enjoy posting photos and want to stay active online, there are ways to do so while maintaining your privacy.

Go ahead to share images that capture random aspects of your life but keep the messages vague and non-specific. For instance, you might post a photo of a hand holding a coffee mug at a café, a scenic view of the city, or a luggage bag at the airport. Accompany these pictures with ambiguous captions like, "Getting there," "My view," "Thanks for the coffee," "About last night," or "Hey you."

These types of posts enable you to remain active on social media while keeping the focus on general moments rather than detailed updates about your personal life. This strategy helps manage curiosity and preserves your privacy, allowing you to maintain an online presence without oversharing.

Lastly, maintaining a low profile means focusing entirely on yourself. Avoid the temptation to browse through other people's profiles, especially that of your ex. This is your chance to redirect the love and attention you once gave to someone else back towards yourself. Embrace this period as an opportunity to nurture your own well-being and self-worth.

As mentioned earlier, consider changing your hair color, trying a new hairstyle, or altering your appearance in any way that excites you. The key is to make this process enjoyable and not a chore. It's perfectly normal to feel some hesitation at first, and that's okay—choose changes that align with your comfort and personal style.

Transforming your appearance can be a powerful way to shift your attitude and boost your confidence. This isn't about adopting a new persona but about enhancing the one you already have. Aim for a fresh attitude that sets you apart and helps you stand out from the crowd. Embrace this change as a way to celebrate your beauty and intelligence. You are more than deserving of feeling extraordinary and confident in your own skin.

Examples of keeping a low profile

1. **Dress Up and Explore:** Treat yourself to an adventure by visiting a new place you've never been before. Enjoy this experience solo and keep it to yourself. It's a wonderful opportunity to focus on your own company and discover new interests.

2. **Update Your Social Media Profile:** Temporarily replace your profile photo with a neutral or random image. Avoid using memes or photos that might seem like indirect messages to your ex. This change helps you

maintain privacy and prevents unnecessary speculation.

3. **Share the Spotlight:** If you choose to go out with friends, let them take and post the photos. This way, you can still enjoy social moments without being directly involved in the online sharing.

4. **Take a Social Media Break:** Consider stepping away from social media altogether. If you're up for it, temporarily disable your account to resist the urge to check in and stay focused on your personal growth.

5. **Discover a New Hobby:** Dive into activities you enjoy or explore new hobbies. Engaging in something you love not only keeps you busy but might also reveal talents you didn't know you

Let's Review

- **What do you think about keeping a low profile?**

Keeping a low profile can be a powerful strategy for maintaining your privacy and focusing on self-growth. By limiting your social media presence and personal disclosures, you can manage curiosity, avoid unnecessary drama, and create space for your own transformation. Reflect on how stepping back from public scrutiny can help you concentrate on personal development and emotional healing.

✓ **What is your takeaway from this chapter?**

The key takeaway from this chapter is the importance of protecting your personal space and focusing on yourself during challenging times. Embracing a low profile allows you to redefine your identity and confidence without external pressures. It's a time to nurture your own well-being, explore new interests, and avoid distractions that might hinder your growth. Use this period to build a stronger, more self-assured version of yourself.

Chapter 4

Hobby Time

Get busy!

Staying busy is one of the most effective ways to navigate a breakup. Here's why:

Consider this: What are you truly passionate about? Is there something you've always wanted to pursue but never had the chance to? Now is the perfect time to dive into those interests and hobbies. Engaging in activities you genuinely enjoy can be incredibly fulfilling and provide a positive distraction during this period.

However, it's important to choose hobbies that you love. If you pick something just because it seems productive but lacks enthusiasm for it, you're likely to lose interest quickly. Think of it like exercise—people often start working out with the goal of losing weight or improving health, but if they don't have a genuine passion for it, they eventually lose motivation and fall back into old habits.

By focusing on activities that excite you, you'll not only stay occupied but also find joy and purpose. Embrace this time to rediscover and invest in what you truly love, and you'll find that it helps you heal and grow beyond the breakup.

One of my favorite hobbies is shopping. I don't necessarily need a budget to enjoy a shopping trip—just the thrill of exploring the latest interior designs, home décor, and fashion brings me joy. It's what inspired my passion for remodeling homes and gardening. What about you?

Find something that genuinely interests you and start there. Research ways to enhance your experience in that hobby. If it requires more money than you currently have, consider whether it's feasible to save up for it. If not, explore alternative hobbies that are more budget friendly.

The main goal of immersing yourself in hobbies is to keep your mind occupied and to facilitate healing. Many hobbies demand time and focus, which can help distract you from overthinking and provide a sense of accomplishment. Additionally, engaging in these activities often uncovers hidden talents and qualities you may not have known you possessed.

Maintaining good mental health is crucial, especially during challenging times. By investing in hobbies that you love, you not only distract yourself from the pain but also discover new ways to bring happiness and fulfillment into your life.

List of hobbies you can try

Gardening: I've dabbled in gardening before and found it to be a truly peaceful hobby. It does require time and dedication, but the rewards are well worth it. Gardening isn't limited to just planting trees; you can explore various aspects such as decorating your garden, researching medicinal plants, or even growing your own fruits and vegetables. It's a fantastic way to connect with nature and create a serene space. If you believe that gardening sounds like fun and you want to try it but don't know how to start, please refer to page

<u>Remodeling a Room or Home:</u> Remodeling can be a time-consuming endeavor, but it's incredibly fulfilling if it's something you're passionate about. Whether you're working with small spaces or tackling a larger project, the process of transforming a space can be immensely satisfying. Take your time with the project and enjoy the journey of making a space uniquely yours. The longer and more detailed the process, the more rewarding it can be. (See more on page 173)

<u>Art</u>

If you have a knack for color and design, give painting a try. Start with basic supplies like paper, paint, and brushes. Let your emotions guide your brushstrokes and see where your creativity takes you. Art can be a powerful form of expression, and many successful artists began as amateurs just experimenting. If painting isn't your thing, you might also enjoy collecting art. The key is to find what resonates with you and brings you joy.

<u>Cooking</u>

Cooking is a fantastic hobby, especially if you enjoy experimenting with flavors and creating new dishes. With countless recipes available online and through cookbooks, you can explore various cuisines and techniques. Start with basic recipes and gradually add your own twists to make the dishes uniquely yours. Cooking for yourself and others can be incredibly rewarding. For inspiration, check out cooking shows and food blogs—

there's always something new to learn and try.

Traveling and Meeting People

Traveling is a wonderful way to broaden your horizons and meet new people. Whether you're exploring nearby cities or venturing to distant countries, every journey offers a chance to learn about different cultures and make new friends. Budget accordingly and choose destinations that excite you. Establishing connections with people from other places can make your travels more memorable and motivate you to return. Remember, the best trips often involve visiting friends and creating lasting bonds.

Planning Parties

If you have a flair for organization and enjoy lively social events, party planning could be a perfect hobby for you. Offer to help friends with their upcoming events by researching venues, rental equipment, or catering options. Event planning can be a lot of fun, and it might even open doors to exciting career opportunities. Check out online resources for bargains on event supplies and consider creating unique, personalized touches for the parties you plan. This can not only enhance your skills but also potentially lead to extra income.

Sewing

Sewing isn't just for professionals or clothing. With beginner-friendly sewing machines and instructional guides, you can start creating a variety of projects. If making clothes doesn't appeal to you, try crafting placemats, simple home décor items, or other small projects. As you gain skills and confidence, you might even turn your creations into small businesses.

Pottery

Pottery is a wonderfully hands-on and creative hobby. While it can get a bit messy, the process of molding clay into functional and decorative pieces is both relaxing and rewarding. You can create personalized mugs, plates, and various crafts. It's a fantastic way to express your creativity and make unique gifts for yourself and others.

Scrapbooking

Scrapbooking is a fantastic way to preserve memories and express your creativity. Scrapbooking allows you to combine photographs, mementos, and artistic elements to create personalized keepsakes. It's more than just a craft; it's a way to document your life's important moments, stories, and experiences in a visually appealing and meaningful way.

Photography

Photography offers a unique way to see and share the world around you. It's a means of self-expression, a way to document your experiences, and an opportunity to explore different perspectives. Whether you're capturing a beautiful sunset, a candid moment with friends, or the details of everyday life, photography helps you tell stories through images.

Let's recap.

What captures your attention for an extended period?

Consider what activities or interests keep you engaged and excited. Reflect on the hobbies or projects that have consistently held your focus in the past. This could be anything from creative pursuits, physical activities, or intellectual challenges.

Overview of a few things you might want to try:

1. Gardening – Creating a beautiful outdoor space or growing your own vegetables.

2. Photography – Capturing moments, experimenting with different styles and techniques.

3. Cooking – Trying new recipes and perfecting your culinary skills.

4. Painting or Drawing – Expressing yourself through art and exploring different mediums.

5. Sewing – Making your own clothes or home décor items.

6. Dancing – Learning new dance styles or taking dance classes.

7. Pottery – Crafting unique pieces and experimenting with shapes and glazes.

8. Traveling – Exploring new places and meeting new people.

9. Event Planning – Organizing parties, events, and getting creative with themes.

10. Scrapbooking – Preserving memories in a creative and personalized way.

Get busy!

Start with one or two of these activities that resonate most with you. Dive in and give them a fair try. Remember, the goal is to engage in activities that you enjoy and that help you grow. If one hobby doesn't quite fit, don't be discouraged—simply move on to the next one on your list. The key is to stay active and keep discovering what brings you joy and satisfaction.

Notes

Chapter 5
Travel. Full. Stop.

Ladies, you truly haven't experienced the richness of life until you've embarked on a journey of solo travel. And I'm not just talking about a vacation with family/friends but stepping out on your own for pure adventure and self-discovery.

Let me share a bit of my own journey to explain what I mean.

I've had the privilege of traveling to Cuba in the Caribbean multiple times, and each visit has been nothing short of transformative. In Cuba, I didn't just see a new place; I met people who became like family. The vibrant culture, the tantalizing dishes, and the extraordinary talent I encountered there were eye-opening. The atmosphere in Cuba is all about fun and adventure, and the warmth of the people can lift even the heaviest of spirits.

There was a time, particularly after my separation, when I found myself consumed by sadness and frustration. I would sit at home, overwhelmed by thoughts of how someone could be so callous abandoning their family, starting new relationships, and leaving behind a heartbroken spouse with three children. The weight of these thoughts was heavy, and I needed an escape.

That's when I turned to travel. Exploring new places and immersing myself in different cultures became my solace. It wasn't just about getting away; it was about discovering new facets of myself and finding joy in the unknown. It helped me break free from the cycle of negative thinking and opened up a world of possibilities.

f you're feeling stuck or overwhelmed, a solo trip might just be what you need. It doesn't have to be a grand adventure; even a local getaway can provide the rejuvenation you're seeking. The essence is to embrace the adventure, let go of your worries, and allow yourself to be uplifted by new experiences and interactions.

Traveling proved to be incredibly effective for me during a challenging period. I was caught in a cycle of overthinking, which led to losing my appetite, sleep, and even weight. It became clear that while I was struggling, my ex was seemingly thriving, and the children remained unaware of the turmoil I was facing. To make matters worse, I was subjected to relentless gossip from neighbors about my ex and his new relationships—comments that were both painful and uninvited.

I needed a way to escape and heal, and that's when I turned to travel. Cuba became my sanctuary. The relief was immediate. My mind cleared as I immersed myself in the vibrant sights and sounds of the island. Exploring museums, art galleries, and attending captivating shows like the 'Tropicana Show' or a lively cabaret was transformative. These experiences provided a fresh perspective and a much-needed respite from my troubles.

If you're feeling weighed down, consider embarking on a solo journey to reclaim your peace and joy. It's a chance to explore new aspects of yourself and find solace in unfamiliar surroundings. For me, traveling became a powerful tool for healing. Beyond my adventures in Cuba, I also frequented America. I recall moments of confusion and isolation, feeling ashamed and alone. But through it all, I learned to navigate life independently, with guidance from God.

One of my favorite destinations was Fort Lauderdale, from where I would drive to Orlando. Those long drives allowed me to clear my mind and appreciate the changing scenery. Once in Orlando, I indulged in shopping, discovering that it could be incredibly therapeutic. If you haven't been to Orlando, I highly recommend it. The city is home to numerous outlets with fantastic discounts on top brands, and the attractions are a great motivation to explore. Although the hotels can be pricey, staying at one that offers breakfast made the expense worthwhile. It gave me the luxury of sleeping in without the hassle of finding breakfast.

Here's a piece of advice: "Shop until you drop" isn't just a catchy phrase—it's a supplement for self-care. When you're in a relationship, it's wise to save some of your money for those rainy days when you need retail therapy to lift your spirits. Shopping can be a powerful way to cope and heal, making it a valuable tool for any woman navigating the challenges of a break-up.

However, shopping isn't the only way to find therapy during your travels. Consider treating yourself to a day at a luxurious spa, dining at a top-notch restaurant, or booking a comfortable hotel room for a solo retreat. These experiences can provide a much-needed escape and rejuvenation.

Here's a little tip: while you're still in the relationship, it's wise to set aside some of the money your partner gives you for yourself. Create a separate account and make regular deposits—this way, you'll have a financial cushion for those times when you need a little extra support.

In summary, use your own funds to embark on trips and engage in activities that bring you joy. Don't waste your time dwelling on past events or spending your days in sorrow. Embrace the healing power of travel and self-care, and remember, you deserve to be pampered and to enjoy life to its fullest.

Finally, it's crucial to be honest with yourself about your feelings. If you haven't truly moved on and are still struggling with the breakup, acknowledge it. Denying your emotions or pretending you're over someone when you're not will only delay your healing process. Admitting where you are emotionally is the first step towards seeking the help and support you need. Recognize that healing is a journey, and being truthful with yourself is essential to finding the path forward and eventually moving on.

Meeting People during travel

Traveling can be a refreshing and transformative experience when done with the right intentions. It's important to approach it as an opportunity to enrich your life, not to distract yourself with temporary pleasures or to chase after new relationships. Focus on exploring new places, making genuine connections, and immersing yourself in different cultures. Enjoy local cuisine, embark on adventures, and embrace your newfound freedom.

I recall a trip to New York with my sister, where we stayed in Jersey and ventured into Manhattan late at night. It was my first visit, and I was completely unprepared for the sheer vibrancy and energy of the city. The experience was eye-opening and exhilarating, reminding me of the endless possibilities that travel can offer. Let your journeys be about discovering new aspects of the world and yourself, not about escaping your past.

Everything around me was vibrant and alive, just like something out of a movie. The streets were bustling with people, and the energy was palpable. I was amazed by how the city was exactly like the scenes you see on TV—shops, hotels, and businesses were everywhere, creating an overwhelming yet exhilarating atmosphere.

One of the highlights was the rail train with its open-air concept, and riding the subway for the first time was a unique experience. We used it to travel daily from Jersey into New York, and it quickly became a favorite part of our trip.

I was thrilled beyond words, especially when I saw the multi-story department stores with each floor dedicated to different fashion trends and colors. I fell in love with their concept immediately. Even though I ended up maxing out my card, the experience was worth every penny. The city's endless hustle and bustle truly lives up to its reputation as the city that never sleeps. If you ever get the chance, I highly recommend visiting—it's an unforgettable experience!

Traveling is a great way to lift your spirits and find joy, but it's important to manage your budget wisely. I encourage you to invest your money in experiences that truly bring you happiness and relaxation. I once knew someone who traveled to her favorite destination, where she enjoyed the luxury of a maid, a comfortable stay, and affordable costs. She felt like royalty and found a perfect place of comfort for herself.

If you're looking for ideas, here are a few destinations worth considering:

1. **Alberta, Canada**: Stay at a hotel near Banff and explore Banff National Park. The scenery is breathtaking, with highlights like Lake Louise and numerous hiking trails.

2. **Toronto, Canada**: Enjoy shopping at the Eaton Center and take a day trip to Niagara Falls. For some excitement, visit Clifton Hill, known for its fun and games.

3. **Europe**: Europe offers a diverse range of experiences. Travel through the Chunnel from England to Paris, visit the Fjords and Cliffs of Moher in Ireland, and explore

Barcelona's La Sagrada Familia, an unfinished church with a fascinating history by architect Antoni Gaudi. In Scotland, the Scottish Highlands provide stunning views, and you can cruise Loch Ness, visit historic castles, and stroll along the Royal Mile.

4. Asia offers a stunning array of destinations for every type of traveler. The Maldives, with its pristine white-sand beaches and crystal-clear waters, provides a serene escape in the Indian Ocean. For a blend of bustling city life and rich cultural experiences, Japan is ideal. Tokyo's vibrant shopping districts are a must-visit, offering everything from cutting-edge fashion to traditional goods. Bali, Indonesia, is perfect for those looking to reconnect with nature, with its lush

landscapes and tranquil atmosphere. For the adventurous, a journey to see Mount Everest promises breathtaking views of some of the world's highest peaks.

In China, the Great Wall offers a historical adventure with stunning vistas, while Hong Kong's dynamic cityscape combines modernity with rich cultural traditions. Thailand is another essential destination; its beautiful temples, delicious street food, and lively night markets provide a rich tapestry of experiences. Each of these destinations offers a unique glimpse into the diverse cultures and landscapes of Asia, making them unforgettable stops on any travel itinerary.

5. **Australia** is a captivating destination with diverse experiences to offer. In Sydney, you can marvel at the iconic Sydney Opera House and, for an extra thrill, take on the Sydney Harbour Bridge Climb for panoramic city views. Bondi Beach, known for its golden sands and surf, provides the perfect spot for relaxation. Moving north, the Great Barrier Reef presents an unparalleled underwater adventure, with snorkeling and diving revealing vibrant coral reefs and marine life. The nearby Whitsunday Islands, with their stunning beaches, including the famous Whitehaven Beach, are a dream getaway.

   Melbourne, renowned for its vibrant street art and café culture, invites you to explore its laneways and enjoy its Royal Botanic Gardens. A scenic drive along the Great Ocean Road showcases breathtaking coastal views and the impressive Twelve Apostles rock formations. In Tasmania, the Cradle Mountain-Lake St Clair National Park offers pristine wilderness perfect for hiking, while Hobart's historic charm and the lively Salamanca Market add to the city's appeal. Finally, a visit to Uluru (Ayers Rock) provides a profound cultural experience, allowing you to connect with the Indigenous significance of this majestic monolith and enjoy its stunning sunrise and sunset vistas. Australia's varied landscapes—from bustling cities and serene beaches to rugged outback and lush rainforests—ensure a memorable experience for every traveler.

6. The Caribbean offers an enchanting array of islands, each with its own distinct charm and allure. From the vibrant culture to the stunning natural beauty, every island presents a unique experience. Whether you're exploring the pristine white sandy beaches, savoring a refreshing daiquiri, or immersing yourself in local hotspots, the Caribbean promises a blend of adventure, relaxation, and pampering. Wander through picturesque landscapes, bask in the warm sun, and embrace the laid-back island vibe. The memories you make in these idyllic settings will stay with you long after your visit.

For the latest in travel news, trends, and must-visit destinations, here are some great resources:

Instagram Pages:

- ✓ Onvigo_inc
- ✓ Onvigo.inosia.milfort
- ✓ BaxterMediaca
- ✓ Beautiful Places
- ✓ Beautiful Destinations
- ✓ Beautiful Hotels
- ✓ Best Vacations
- ✓ Travel Caribbean
- ✓ JetSetSarah

Facebook Pages:

- ✓ Cruise Hive
- ✓ World of Travel and Food

- ✓ Luxury Travel Advisor
- ✓ Travel Agent Magazine
- ✓ Cruise Critic
- ✓ The Travel Agent Next Door

These pages offer a wealth of information and inspiration to help you plan your next adventure.

***Secret**: Traveling alone is like having a VIP pass to your own adventure. Think of it this way: you get to decide the itinerary, choose the local spots, and indulge in every quirky food you stumble upon without anyone judging your choice of a mystery meat dish. Plus, there's no one to argue with about whether to visit the museum or the beach—you can do both and still have room for a nap! Solo travel means you get to enjoy the* *freedom to be as spontaneous or as lazy as you want. Want to take a million selfies or eat dessert for every meal? Go for it. Enjoy your journey, and don't forget to snap some photos that might make your friends question their own travel choices!*

NOTES

After diving into those amazing travel resources, are you itching to pack your bags? The world is brimming with stunning destinations just waiting for you to explore. Jot down up to ten places that have sparked your interest and get ready to plan your next epic adventure.

_____

_____

_____

_____

_____

_____

_____

_____

CHAPTER 6
BECOME A BOSS

If I had to choose between a man and my career, I'd pick my career faster than you can say "promotion." Some might think that's cold, but after navigating the wild rollercoaster of relationships, I'm as certain as I am that Mondays are tough—I'd be making the right call.

Here's the deal: choose your career. Why? Because there's nothing quite like the thrill of spending your own hard-earned money on something fabulous. Sure, it's nice to splurge on a luxury item with someone else's cash, but I'd rather not spend my life waiting for Mr. Wallet to come through. Plus, the mystery of what he's thinking about you—besides "Where's my money?"—can be a real mood killer.

Let's be honest: money can be a relationship deal-breaker. When it starts to feel like every date is a financial negotiation, it's no wonder couples end up calling it quits. So, keep your career close, your wallet closer, and let's be real—there's no such thing as too many new pairs of shoes!

I'm not proclaiming that we should treat all men the same but choosing a career over a relationship—or vice versa—depends on individual values and life goals. Following are some reasons why one might want to focus on a career rather than chasing a man:

1. Financial Independence: A stable career provides financial security and independence. Relying on someone else for money can create dependency and tension. Having your own income means you can make choices based on what you want, not just what you can afford.

2. Personal Fulfillment: Many people find great satisfaction in pursuing their passions and achieving career goals. This sense of accomplishment can be deeply fulfilling and can contribute to overall happiness.

3. Autonomy: A career allows for personal and professional growth. You have control

over your own decisions and the direction of your life, which can be empowering.

4. Future Stability: A well-established career can offer long-term stability and benefits that might be more difficult to achieve in a relationship, especially if the relationship faces challenges.

5. Avoiding Financial Conflict: Financial issues can be a significant source of stress in relationships. Having your own career can minimize these conflicts and reduce the risk of money-related strain.

6. Growth and Self-Discovery: Investing time and energy in your career can lead to personal growth and self-discovery. This can enhance your sense of identity and

confidence, which can positively impact all areas of your life, including relationships.

7. Shifting Priorities: At different stages of life, priorities shift. Early in a career, the focus might be on building skills and achieving goals, while later, one might prioritize different aspects of life, including relationships.

Ultimately, the choice between a career and a relationship is deeply personal and varies based on individual circumstances. It's about finding a balance that aligns with your values, goals, and what brings you the most happiness and fulfillment.

So, you're itching to make some cash but don't have a trade or business degree? No problem! First things first: What are you interested in? Are you a genius at whipping up new ideas? When it comes to making money, don't underestimate your talents. The world is overflowing with the same old, same old, but people love fresh, creative inventions.

Got a talent? Use it! Think of it as seasoning—your natural skills plus a sprinkle of innovation equals something truly unique. Dive into your creative process, experiment until you're doing a happy dance, and then— voila! —you've got your invention.

Now, it's time to play detective. Hit the web and see if your creation has any look-alikes. Check out the competition, see how they're pricing their stuff, and then set your price accordingly. Remember, if it's worth creating, it's worth pricing right.

And here's a bonus: While you're diving into this creative whirlwind, you'll be so absorbed in your inventive journey that you'll barely have time to think about those pesky relationship issues. Who has time for drama when you're busy making extra cash?

If you're sitting, laying or standing there thinking, "Talent? What talent?" don't worry—you're not alone! Sometimes, finding your hidden ability feels like searching for a needle in a haystack. But fear not, help is at hand! Below, I've got a list of websites and books to help you uncover that undiscovered touch of talent.

Think of these resources as your personal talent scout. They're like having a GPS for discovering your hidden skills. Dive into these gems, and you might just find that your next big idea is hiding in plain sight.

And remember, even if you don't find a hidden talent, you'll at least have some fun exploring. So, grab a cup of coffee, get cozy, and let these tools guide you on your quest for brilliance!

Money Making Websites:

Freelancing Platforms

1. Upwork – Offers a wide range of freelance jobs, from writing and graphic design to programming and consulting.

2. <u>Fiverr</u> – A platform where you can offer services (or "gigs") starting at $5. Great for creative and digital services.

3. <u>Freelancer</u> – Connects freelancers with clients needing various services, including writing, design, and coding.

Gig Economy & Microtasks

1. <u>Amazon Mechanical Turk</u> – Provides microtasks like data entry, surveys, and simple online tasks that pay small amounts.

2. <u>TaskRabbit</u> – Offers opportunities for local tasks, such as running errands or assembling furniture. (Note: TaskRabbit is more location-based.)

Selling and Reselling

1. Etsy – Ideal for selling handmade crafts, vintage items, and digital products.

2. eBay – Perfect for selling new and used items. Great for decluttering or reselling.

Content Creation & Monetization

1. YouTube – Create videos and earn money through ads, sponsorships, and merchandise.

2. Twitch – Stream video games or other content and make money through subscriptions, donations, and sponsorships.

Online Surveys & Market Research

1. <u>Swagbucks</u> – Earn points by taking surveys, watching videos, and shopping online, which can be redeemed for gift cards or cash.

2. <u>Survey Junkie</u> – Participate in surveys and get paid for your opinions.

Teaching & Tutoring

1. <u>VIPKid</u> – Teach English to children in China from the comfort of your home.

2. <u>Teachable</u> – Create and sell online courses on any subject you're knowledgeable about.

Investing & Trading

1. <u>Robinhood</u> – A user-friendly platform for trading stocks and cryptocurrencies with no commission fees.

2. <u>Coinbase</u> – A popular platform for buying, selling, and managing cryptocurrencies.

Each of these platforms has its own set of requirements and opportunities, so it's worth exploring a few to see which best matches your skills and interests!

Books for Financial Empowerment and Success for Women

1. *Girl, Stop Apologizing: A Shame-Free Plan for Embracing and Achieving Your Goals* by Rachel Hollis
Hollis provides motivation and practical advice for women to overcome self-doubt and pursue their goals, including financial independence.

2. *The Total Money Makeover: A Proven Plan for Financial Fitness* by Dave Ramsey
While not exclusively for women, this book offers a clear, step-by-step plan for financial health and wealth-building that many women find empowering.

3. *Women & Money: Owning the Power to Control Your Destiny* by Suze Orman
   Suze Orman provides practical financial advice specifically tailored to women, addressing common financial challenges and empowering women to take control of their finances.

4. *Broke Millennial: Stop Scraping By and Get Your Financial Life Together* by Erin Lowry
   This book offers practical advice on managing money, paying off debt, and investing, all aimed at helping young women build a solid financial foundation.

5. *The Confidence Code: The Science and Art of Self-Assurance—What Women Should Know* by Katty Kay and Claire Shipman
   While not solely about money, this book

explores the role of confidence in career and financial success, offering insights into how women can harness their self-assurance to achieve their goals.

6. *Dare to Lead: Brave Work. Tough Conversations. Whole Hearts.* by Brené Brown
Brown's book on leadership and courage is essential for women looking to excel in their careers and take charge of their financial futures.

7. *Powerful: Building a Culture of Freedom and Responsibility* by Patty McCord
McCord shares her experiences and insights on leadership and creating a positive work environment, which can be invaluable for

women entrepreneurs and career-driven individuals.

NOTES: There are so many more to choose from. What are three steps you feel you may take toward your next goal

_____

_____

_____

_____

_____

_____

_____

CHAPTER 7

SET GOALS AND WIN

Everyone should have at least one goal they're excited to crush. Why not take a moment to think about your goals and start looking forward to achieving them? There's nothing quite like the thrill of anticipation, especially when you know you're on track to make it happen. It's like having a victory party in your mind before the actual celebration begins.

Sure, the wait can sometimes feel like an endless loop of anxiety, but wouldn't you rather deal with the stress of waiting than worry about something you're not even close to accomplishing? Life is all about choosing our battles wisely. Sometimes, fighting for too long just wears us out, and it feels easier to throw in the towel.

Think about it like this: Have you ever watched someone in a fighting game decide to stop fighting? Spoiler alert—it doesn't end well. The player who quits gets pummeled and loses the match. Life is no different. If you give up and stop trying, you risk losing everything you've worked for, including your chance at happiness.

So, if you ever feel like giving up, don't throw in the towel just yet. Instead, hit pause. Take a breather, reassess, and then hit play when you're ready. After all, sometimes all you need is a little break to come back stronger and ready to tackle your goals head-on!

Take a moment to hit pause and review your life. Think about those dreams and aspirations you've always had but never had the chance to pursue. Grab a pen and paper—yes, the classic kind! There's something powerful about putting your thoughts down on paper. Even scripture gets it right; Habakkuk 2:2 (King James Version) says, *"And the Lord answered me, and said, Write the vision, and make it plain upon tables, that he may run that readeth it."* Essentially, write it down so you can see it, understand it and chase it down until you get it!

Your goals are your vision. Only you know how fiercely you want to achieve them and what it will take to get there. For those of us navigating through pain and disappointment, it's crucial that our goals focus on rebuilding and empowering ourselves.

Set goals that not only make you a better version of yourself but also refine and define your character. Aim to be smarter, wiser, and wealthier—not just financially but emotionally and spiritually too. It's common to focus on healing when you're hurting, but remember time heals, and taking positive steps now can pave the way for a brighter future.

If you're reading this, it's clear you're on a journey to overcome some deep pain. Embrace that process and channel your energy into goals that will transform your life. Healing is not just about moving past the pain—it's about setting new visions and making them a reality. So, get those goals down on paper, and let's get moving towards a future where you're thriving!

I understand firsthand that the journey through heartache is challenging, but the good news is that healing does come with time. So, make it a goal to focus on taking one day at a time. It's about finding small victories and keeping hope alive as you navigate through the pain toward success.

Here are some targets to consider as you move forward, one step at a time:

1. *Self-Care Routine*: Establish a daily self-care routine that makes you feel good. This could include things like going to a spa, journaling, reading the word of God or simply taking time to relax and unwind.

2. **Learning and Growth:** Set a goal to learn something new or develop a new skill. Whether it's picking up a new hobby, taking an online course, or reading a book, investing in yourself can be incredibly empowering.

3. **Reconnect with Passion:** Identify activities or interests that bring you joy and make a plan to reconnect with them. Rediscovering your passions can help reignite your sense of

purpose and happiness. Mine has always been cooking, writing and remodeling.

4. **Healthy Relationships:** Focus on nurturing and building positive relationships with friends and family. Remember surrounding yourself with supportive people can make a big difference in your recovery.

5. **Physical Wellness:** Incorporate exercise and healthy eating into your routine. Physical health can greatly impact your emotional well-being and give you more energy to face each day.

6. **Set Small, Achievable Goals:** Break down your larger goals into smaller, manageable tasks. Celebrate your progress, no matter

how small, and use each success as motivation to keep moving forward.

7. **Mindfulness and Reflection:** Make time for mindfulness and reflection. Understanding and processing your emotions can be a crucial part of healing and personal growth.

Taking it one day at a time, these goals can help you create a path forward, allowing you to build a fulfilling and joyful life as you heal. Keep moving forward, and remember that progress, no matter how small, is still progress.

Other Goals

1. Find the courage to get up and function normally

2. Make meeting new people a part of your day

3. Set travel goals to places you have never been

4. Start a new hobby

5. Dare yourself to look better and change your appearance suddenly

6. Join a gym

7. Commit to listening to jokes in the morning or throughout your day

8. Make yourself think of anything that makes you smile

NOTES: What are some goals you've been dreaming about but haven't had the chance to start yet? List them out and consider what steps you need to take to kick things off.

_____

_____

_____

_____

_____

_____

_____

CHAPTER 8

A SURVEY ABOUT WHY MEN LEAVE

If you were to ask a man why he ended a relationship, you might hear a familiar story: it often boils down to blaming the woman for something she did—or didn't do.

Here's a thought: if men can recognize issues in the relationship, why not address them openly? Why not guide their partner on what's wrong or right? To answer these questions, we need to acknowledge that men and women perceive and communicate differently. The way a man views a situation and the way he expresses it can be quite different from a woman's perspective. This disconnect can make it difficult to convey messages effectively, leading each side to feel misunderstood or uncared for.

To get a clearer picture, I conducted a survey with ten men from diverse backgrounds—Italian, South American, North American, Caribbean, Canadian, Asian, and African, ranging in age from 24 to 50. The survey aimed to explore their perspectives on breakups and to gauge whether they truly care about the pain experienced by their partners.

The responses were eye-opening and remarkably honest. However, to avoid stereotyping, it's important to remember that not all men think alike. Each individual is unique. What's valuable here is gaining insight into how some men perceive these issues.

Question 1 *What do you think about women crying?*

Answer: All of the men responded respectfully to the question. Some laughed, while others took a moment to reflect before answering. The majority, however, had a common reaction: "I don't understand why women cry so much." One man offered a more empathetic perspective. He shared that when his girlfriend cries during an argument or a heated discussion, he feels compelled to comfort her. Yet, once the immediate emotional storm subsides, he finds himself shutting down and withdrawing. This reveals that sometimes, emotions can be a barrier to open communication, leading to unspoken feelings and hidden issues.

Question 2 *How do you handle a breakup?*

Answer: "*I go my way so she could go her way.*" Nine out of ten men agreed that if a woman initiates a breakup, they want to know the reason behind it. They briefly mentioned that they suspect she might have someone else in mind. On the other hand, six out of ten men said that if they were the ones ending the relationship, they hope the woman would understand and move on quickly. It seems that while they seek clarity when they are on the receiving end, they are less inclined or unable to offer the same level of understanding and openness when the roles are reversed.

Question 3 *Would you consider giving your ex another chance at the relationship?*

Answer: They all agreed that they would be willing to give their exes a second chance, but only if they still had strong feelings for the woman. They also expressed the belief that some women can be quite challenging to deal with.

Question 4 *What are your thoughts on a staying in touch after a breakup?*

Answer: When it comes to keeping in touch with an ex, all ten men agreed that it would be frustrating to have to deal with someone after making it clear. They need space. One man acknowledged that breakups are painful but noted that constant nagging only makes matters worse. Another agreed that giving each other space to reflect and decide on the next steps is the best approach. Another individual expressed a desire to be the one to pursue his ex, stating, "Let me be the one to go after you and beg you to come back"— highlighting his preference for taking the initiative in rekindling the relationship.

Question 5 *How do you handle a breakup?*

Answer: They all acknowledged that women are likely to cry during a breakup although there are some others who would prefer to pretend they are fine. They mentioned that they prepare themselves to handle this emotional response. Their consensus was that they want women to understand and accept that the relationship is over, and to come to terms with it.

Question 6 *What do you believe cause breakups?*

The answers varied, with reasons including financial issues, misunderstandings (#1), cheating, and false accusations.

Question 7 *What do you think about strong women?*

Answer: All the men I interviewed expressed a preference for a woman with her own independent mind. One individual remarked that a strong woman is a complement to a man, highlighting the value they place on mutual respect and individuality in a relationship.

Question 8 *Have you ever truly been in love?*

Answer: Regarding being in love, eight out of ten men indicated that they are no longer with the person they first fell in love with.

Question 9 *Are you cold enough to cheat on someone you love?*

Answer: Yeah, (and none of them cracked a smile).

Question 10 *Do you believe you will ever fall in love again the way you did the first time?*

Answer: Seven out of ten men responded that they are unsure.

Disclaimer: Not all men are the same and they certainly do not think the same way. This survey was only based on statistics.

In my recent studies and as a relationship coach, I have found that men may leave a relationship for a variety of reasons, and these reasons can be complex and multifaceted. Some common reasons include:

1. Communication Issues

- **Lack of Effective Communication:** Persistent communication problems can lead to misunderstandings and unresolved conflicts, causing frustration and dissatisfaction.

2. Emotional Disconnect

- **Loss of Emotional Connection:** Over time, some men may feel they have drifted apart from their partner emotionally, leading to a sense of detachment.

3. Unresolved Conflicts

- **Ongoing Disagreements:** Constant arguments or unresolved issues can create a toxic environment, pushing someone to end the relationship.

4. Infidelity

- **Cheating:** Infidelity can severely damage trust and lead to a breakup, as it often signifies deeper issues or a lack of commitment.

5. Personal Growth and Change

- **Changing Priorities:** Individuals evolve, and sometimes their goals, values, or interests diverge significantly from their partner's.

6. Financial Strain

- **Economic Pressures:** Financial problems or differing attitudes towards money can create significant stress and contribute to relationship breakdowns.

7. Lack of Appreciation

- **Feeling Unvalued:** If one partner feels underappreciated or taken for granted, it can lead to resentment and dissatisfaction.

8. Unrealistic Expectations

- **Expectations vs. Reality:** If one partner has expectations that the other cannot meet, it can lead to frustration and disillusionment.

9. Personal Issues

- **Individual Challenges:** Personal issues such as mental health struggles, stress, or unresolved past trauma can affect one's ability to maintain a healthy relationship.

10. Incompatibility

- **Fundamental Differences:** Differences in core values, life goals, or lifestyles can become more apparent over time, leading to a realization that the relationship is no longer viable.

11. Lack of Effort

- **Complacency:** Sometimes, a lack of effort from one or both partners to maintain the relationship can lead to its decline.

12. Desire for Independence

- **Need for Freedom:** Some men may feel the need to explore their independence or personal goals outside of the relationship.

13. External Influences

- **Influence of Friends or Family:** Sometimes, external pressures or opinions from friends or family can impact one's decision to leave a relationship.

14. Loss of Attraction

- **Physical or Emotional Attraction:** Changes in physical appearance, or a loss of emotional or physical attraction, can affect the dynamics of a relationship.

15. Life Changes

- **Significant Life Events:** Major life changes, such as moving to a new city, changing careers, or personal milestones, can alter the relationship's trajectory.

These reasons can often intersect and interact, making each situation unique. Understanding the specific dynamics in any given relationship can help in addressing or preventing potential issues.

CHAPTER 9

DATING OR TALKING TO NEW PEOPLE

Healing takes time, but if you've made it this far in the book, you're definitely strong enough to take this next step.

You may have heard the advice, "To get over someone, start talking to someone new." You might feel that you're not ready or interested in meeting new people right now, and that's perfectly okay. However, talking to others can provide a sense of calm and play a significant role in your healing process.

Taking time to heal from past wounds is essential for your well-being and future happiness. Healing is not a race; it's a personal journey that requires patience and self-compassion. Allow yourself the space to process your emotions, reflect on your experiences, and rebuild your sense of self. Rushing through the healing process or pushing aside your feelings can prolong your recovery and hinder your growth. Embrace this time as an opportunity to learn more about yourself, set new goals, and cultivate resilience. Remember, giving yourself the time to heal is not a sign of weakness, but a crucial step towards becoming stronger and more whole.

For those who are ready to move on, consider this: engaging in conversation doesn't mean you're committing to anything serious.

From my own experience, I know that healing from a breakup often involves grappling with many questions about what went wrong. While it's important to address your feelings, try to avoid overwhelming new acquaintances with too many questions or excessive talk about your past relationship. I've learned that while men do listen (especially to topics that interest them), focusing too much on past grievances might make you seem like someone they could also take advantage of.

So, take it slow, keep the conversation light, and let your interactions help you find a sense of serenity as you continue your path to healing.

Allow the other person to guide the conversation, starting off at a comfortable and relaxed pace. If a topic comes up that you're not ready to discuss, it's perfectly fine to say, "I don't want to talk about that right now." Keep it simple and straightforward.

When you do ask questions, try to keep them non-judgmental. Avoid comparing new people you meet to past partners, especially those who didn't treat you well. Focus on getting to know the person in front of you and let the conversation flow naturally. Sometimes, these interactions can lead to meaningful connections and reveal shared experiences. You might find that the person you're talking to has faced similar challenges or can offer valuable insights based on their own journey.

I once reached a point where I felt an intense aversion to all men. I was so disillusioned that I would avoid any potential suitor, sometimes going so far as to create elaborate excuses to turn them away. Whether a man was handsome, wealthy, or smart, I had convinced myself they were all the same.

Remember, it's natural to feel guarded after a breakup, but allowing yourself to engage with others at your own pace can be a crucial step in your healing process.

One day, I met a police officer who genuinely understood what women go through and could relate to my struggles. As we talked, I discovered that he had his own issues within his relationship. He was determined to save it and sought my perspective on how to address the challenges he was facing. He wanted insights from a woman's point of view.

This experience highlighted what I mentioned earlier: when engaging in conversations, especially with new people, try to avoid bringing up your current relationship issues. Imagine being questioned extensively on how to fix someone else's relationship—

it's overwhelming and a bit surprising. Initially, I was taken aback by his dedication to salvaging his relationship, as it wasn't even a marriage but a informal relationship.

It appeared that his situation was somewhat reversed. There seemed to be past events that led his partner to disengage or pursue her own path. It made me realize that often, underlying issues or past experiences can significantly impact how people approach and handle their current relationships.

I discovered that many men are genuinely willing to work on their relationships. The reality is that they might not always be great at expressing themselves, but they do recognize their mistakes.

However, when meeting new people, it's crucial to be clear about your intentions. If you're only interested in conversation, state that from the start. If you're simply seeking information and not interested in starting anything, let that be known as well.

The man I met was tall, handsome, and young. As I got to know him, I found myself wanting him to be a part of my life. I was impressed by his thoughtful questions and the enthusiasm he displayed about improving his own relationship. His conversations were incredibly helpful to me, lifting a weight from my shoulders. I was grateful to have been able to assist him during my own time of need, and in doing so, I felt like I was helping myself as well.

Starting with small talk is fine, but the conversations often become more engaging as you continue. Keep the dialogue flowing by discussing shared interests and activities you both enjoy. There's a whole world of topics to explore instead of sitting at home feeling frustrated and upset. Remember, your ex is likely not dwelling on how they hurt you, especially if they were the one who ended things. They've moved on, so it's time for you to do the same.

Take a proactive step by treating yourself to a nice lunch occasionally. Embrace the opportunity to be yourself and reconnect with the world. The first step is to get out of your house—no one is going to come knocking on your door to meet you. Dress up and smile because God made you beautiful.

Once you're comfortable being out in the world as a single person, find a favorite restaurant or quiet area where you can relax and think about how blessed you are. Over time, as you become a familiar face in that place, you'll find that people will start to notice you and greet you with respect – making you feel special.

For others, making new friends can happen through travel or recreational activities. As mentioned earlier, even joining a gym can led to meeting someone who's eager to assist you with your workouts. The key takeaway is that you won't meet new people while sitting at home, crying, watching TV, or dwelling on past regrets.

Meeting People Online

I must admit that I've tried various online dating platforms in the past, hoping to find someone meaningful to connect with. Unfortunately, I quickly became disillusioned and learned from the experience. There was no way to verify whether people were genuine, and I encountered all types of individuals, including married men seeking to engage in inappropriate behavior. I made a point not to get involved with such activities, always considering how I would feel if I were in their spouse's position.

If you're looking for advice on casual encounters or hookups, this book is not the right resource. I do not support or encourage such behavior and focus instead on fostering genuine, respectful God sent connections.

Waiting on God, Why Wait?

Waiting on God for a partner is a journey that many find both challenging and rewarding. It's a process that involves trust, patience, and a deep belief that what's meant for you will come in its own time. Choosing to wait rather than rushing into a relationship can save you from repeating past mistakes and help you build a foundation for a healthier and more fulfilling partnership.

When you wait on God, you allow yourself the opportunity to grow and heal from previous experiences. This time can be used for self-discovery, personal development, and strengthening your relationship with yourself. It's a chance to reflect on what you truly want in a partner and in a relationship, and to set clear, healthy boundaries.

Rushing into a relationship often leads to repeating old patterns or settling for less than you deserve. By waiting, you give yourself the space to avoid these pitfalls and to wait for someone who aligns with your values, goals, and needs. This patience can lead to a more meaningful and supportive connection, one that is built on mutual respect and understanding.

Waiting on God also allows you to cultivate a deeper sense of peace and trust. It's a way of acknowledging that there is a plan greater than your own, and that the right person will come along when the time is right. This mindset can help alleviate the anxiety and pressure of finding a partner quickly and can foster a more positive outlook on love and relationships.

Ultimately, waiting for the right partner is about more than just avoiding mistakes; it's about preparing yourself for a relationship that truly enriches your life. It's about believing that love will come in its own time and being ready to embrace it when it does. In this way, waiting can lead to a deeper, more authentic connection that is worth every moment of patience.

Chapter 10

Put God First

In life, we cannot navigate our journey without the involvement of God. He is our Creator and understands how to restore us when we're broken. When you're hurting, turning to your Maker is the most comforting choice. Spend some quiet time with God—cry, pray, and allow Him to heal your wounds. Unlike friends or loved ones, God never tires of your struggles. He is always there for you.

I remember my initial reaction when I discovered my ex was cheating, I turned to

God. At that moment, I wasn't sure what to do, but I instinctively prayed and poured out my anguish to Him. The pain felt like sharp needles piercing my heart. My body was weak, and my mind raced with questions. I sought answers from God, wondering why such suffering was happening to me, despite having been a faithful partner.

Sometimes, life unfolds in ways that defy understanding, and it's not always possible to figure out why things happen the way they do. In those moments of pain and confusion, turning to God provides solace and direction, helping us navigate through the hurt and find healing.

Allow God to heal you and handle the matters of justice on your behalf, but don't spend your life waiting for misfortune to strike your ex. It's important to avoid becoming like many who only turn to God in times of trouble or need. Remember, God is the Creator of the universe, and regardless of your feelings, He is your Father. Including God in your daily life can be incredibly rewarding.

I've found that listening to inspirational figures like Joyce Meyer and Joel Osteen can set a positive tone for your day. They offer guidance on incorporating God into everyday situations and seeing the broader perspective.

I recall a period in my life when I was battling intense mental struggles. My world felt chaotic, but I was fortunate to have a book by Joyce Meyer titled *"The Battlefield of the*

Mind" that someone had gifted me over a decade ago. I revisited it, and the insights I gained were profound. Her advice on managing a wandering mind and focusing on constructive thoughts was particularly helpful. I highly recommend this book, along with others by authors who inspire positive thinking. Make sure to also grab a hold of my next book entitled '*I know It Hurts: Kowing when Its Time To Let Go'*. Good resources can provide valuable encouragement and help you maintain a positive mindset.

The essence of this chapter is to maintain your focus on what truly matters. No one understands you better than the One who created you. It's important to recognize that some people enter our lives for a season, not forever. Relationships work in this way too—God may bring people into our lives for us to learn from or to help us, or vice versa.

From this point forward, make it a priority to put God first in everything. He will guide your path and bless you with success. I speak from experience. When my ex-husband left, I turned to God, seeking strength through prayer and Scripture. By placing my trust in Him for the well-being of my family, I was eventually blessed with a partner who exceeded my expectations. Trusting God for financial stability, a future, a home, and a career led me to receive all these blessings. Everything I have now is a testament to His guidance and provision.

I encourage you to give this approach a try. You have nothing to lose and everything to gain. You don't need to adopt a particular religious label—what matters is starting a personal relationship with your Creator. Open that line of communication, and you may find that your life transforms in ways you never imagined.

Revenge

Imagine moving on with your life, only to find your ex constantly showing up on your dates, trying to tarnish your reputation. Or picture meeting someone who embodies all the qualities you've been longing for—respect, care, generosity, and freedom. It sounds perfect, right? But what if, just as you decide to build a future with this wonderful person, your ex decides to interfere, bringing up past grievances to ruin your happiness? It's understandable if you feel a surge of anger and frustration, but acting on those feelings isn't the solution.

When someone breaks up with us, it's natural to feel hurt, especially when it seems like they've moved on with someone else. The temptation to seek revenge or create chaos to make your pain visible can be overwhelming. However, this approach is not only destructive but ultimately unproductive.

Revenge might offer a fleeting sense of satisfaction, but it rarely leads to a resolution. Often, it results in an ongoing conflict that can escalate and involve others who weren't part of your original relationship. This kind of warfare can spiral out of control and only prolong your suffering.

Instead of seeking revenge, focus on healing and moving forward. Channel your energy into building a fulfilling life and nurturing positive relationships. Revenge rarely brings true peace, while choosing to rise above and focus on your own growth can lead to a more satisfying and lasting sense of victory.

To make a lasting impression and truly move on, focus on yourself and live as if your ex never existed. Show that you are unshaken and maintain your dignity throughout. This is how you send the most powerful message:

"You hoped to break me, but instead, your actions only made me stronger. I'm thriving, and I have you to thank for that."

By prioritizing your own growth and well-being, you demonstrate resilience and self-worth. This approach not only moves you forward but also silently proves that you are unbothered by their attempts to drag you down.

Conclusion

Recovery and Moving On

In this book, we explore the journey of healing and moving forward after a difficult breakup. The central message is that life does not come to an end with the end of a relationship; instead, it offers a new beginning filled with possibilities. We focus on leveraging faith, self-care, and personal growth to navigate this transition.

Key insights include:

1. *Healing Through Faith*: Trust in God's plan for your life and seek His guidance through prayer and reflection. Your faith will provide comfort and direction, transforming your pain into personal growth and success.

2. *Self-Focus and Resilience*: Redirect your focus from past relationships to personal development and self-care. Understand that some people are meant to be in our lives only temporarily. By concentrating on your own goals and well-being, you pave the way for a brighter future.

3. *Navigating Relationships*: When entering new relationships or meeting new people,

approach with clarity and honesty. Avoid bringing unresolved issues from past relationships into new ones and remember that genuine connections are built on mutual respect and understanding.

4. *Avoiding Revenge*: Resist the urge for revenge or to create chaos. Instead, let go of anger and embrace healing. Revenge often perpetuates conflict and prolongs suffering, while focusing on your personal growth brings true peace.

5. *Practical Steps to Move On*: Engage in activities that bring joy and fulfillment. Whether through new hobbies, meaningful conversations, or personal achievements, keep yourself active and positive. Creating

a fulfilling life for yourself demonstrates strength and resilience.

"Remember, life does not end with a breakup; it is an opportunity to start anew. Embrace this chance to reinvent yourself and achieve your goals. Your future holds the promise of happiness and success, and with faith and perseverance, you can build a life that truly reflects your inner strength and potential".

GUIDES AND REFERENCES

Hobbies that you may consider continued

Gardening for beginners Guide

1. Start Small

Begin with a small garden or even just a few pots. This will make it easier to manage and less overwhelming. You can gradually expand as you gain more experience and confidence.

2. Choose Easy-to-Grow Plants

Opt for plants that are known to be beginner-friendly and resilient. Some good choices include:

- *Herbs*: Basil, mint, and chives are simple to grow and useful in cooking.

- *Vegetables*: Lettuce, radishes, and tomatoes are relatively easy and rewarding.

- *Flowers*: Marigolds, sunflowers, and zinnias add color and are typically easy to grow.

3. Understand Your Soil

Good soil is crucial for healthy plants. Start by testing your soil to determine its pH and nutrient levels. You can often buy soil testing kits at garden centers. If your soil needs improvement, consider adding compost or other organic matter to enrich it.

DIY Remodeling Guide

1. Plan Your Project

- *Define Your Goals*: Decide what you want to achieve. Is it more space, better functionality, or a fresh look?

- *Make a List*: Write down all the changes you want to make and prioritize them.

2. Set Your Budget

- *Estimate Costs*: Research the cost of materials and tools you'll need.

- *Include a Buffer*: Set aside extra money for unexpected expenses.

3. Gather Your Tools and Materials

- *Basic Tools*: Hammer, screwdriver, measuring tape, level, utility knife, paintbrushes, and rollers.

- *Materials*: Choose based on your project (e.g., paint, tiles, wood, nails, adhesive).

4. Prepare the Area

- *Clear the Space*: Remove furniture and cover floors with drop cloths.

- *Protect Fixtures*: Tape off areas you don't want to paint or damage.

5. Start with knocking down some stuff (if needed)

- *Safety First***:** Wear gloves, goggles, and a mask.

- *Remove Old Fixtures:* Carefully take out old tiles, cabinets, or any elements you're replacing.

6. Make Necessary Repairs

- *Fix Walls***:** Patch holes and cracks with spackle or drywall compound.

- *Check Plumbing/Electrical***:** If you're making major changes, ensure all systems are in good working order.

7. *Implement Changes*

- *Painting:* Apply primer first if needed. Then, paint your walls, ceilings, or trim.

- *Install New Fixtures***:** Follow manufacturer instructions for installing new lights, faucets, or cabinetry.

8. Update Flooring (if applicable)

- *Remove Old Flooring***:** Take out old carpet or tiles carefully.

- *Install New Flooring***:** Lay down new materials, ensuring they fit well and are properly secured.

9. Add Final Touches

- *Decorate***:** Hang new curtains, add rugs, or set up furniture.

- *Clean Up*: Remove any debris, clean the space thoroughly, and dispose of any waste properly.

Enjoy the results of your hard work and newly remodeled space!

Getting Started with Scrap Booking

1. Gather Materials

Start with basic supplies such as a scrapbook album, decorative papers, stickers, markers, and glue. As you progress, you can add more tools like stamps, washi tape, and embellishments.

2. Organize Your Photos and Mementos

Collect photos, ticket stubs, postcards, and other memorabilia you want to include. Organizing these items before you start will make the process smoother.

3. Design Layouts

Plan the layout of your pages. You can follow themes or create a design that reflects the event or period you're documenting. There's no right or wrong way—let your creativity flow.

4. Add Personal Touches

Write captions, notes, or stories to accompany your photos. This adds context and personal significance to your pages.

5. Experiment and Have Fun

Scrapbooking is a highly personal and flexible hobby. Experiment with different styles, techniques, and materials to find what you enjoy most.

Benefits

- *Creativity:* Scrapbooking allows you to explore your artistic side and experiment with various design techniques.

- *Memory Keeping:* It's a wonderful way to preserve your memories and reflect on important moments in your life.

- *Therapeutic*: The process of scrapbooking can be calming and meditative, offering a break from everyday stresses.

Tips for Success

- *Start Small*: If you're new to scrapbooking, begin with a simple project to build your confidence.

- *Use High-Quality Materials*: Invest in good-quality materials to ensure your scrapbook lasts and looks professional.

- *Join a Community*: Consider joining a scrapbooking group or community, either online or locally, for inspiration and support.

Scrapbooking is not just about creating beautiful pages; it's about making a tangible record of your life's journey. Dive in, have fun, and let your creativity shine!

Getting Started With Photography

1. Explore Different Genres

Try various types of photography, such as landscape, portrait, macro, or street photography, to find what you enjoy most.

2. Invest in Good Equipment

As you advance, consider investing in quality lenses and accessories that enhance your photography experience.

3. Learn from Others

Study the work of other photographers, attend workshops, or take online courses to improve your skills and gain new insights.

4. Be Patient

Great photography takes time and practice. Don't get discouraged by initial challenges; keep learning and growing.

Photography is a hobby that offers endless opportunities for creativity and personal growth. Whether you're capturing stunning landscapes, candid moments, or artistic compositions, each photo tells a story and reflects your unique perspective. Dive into the world of photography and let your imagination and skill shine through your lens

ABOUT THE AUTHOR

Based in Ontario, Canada, I am both a certified relationship coach and a travel advisor. My passion for writing began in childhood, when I would compose heartfelt letters to God. Alongside my love for writing, I enjoy cooking, shopping, reading, and engaging in activities that promote spiritual growth.

As a mother of three very active children, I've learned to navigate the fast-paced world by relying on my faith in God to guide me through challenges and maintain my energy.

This book represents a revised edition of a work originally penned in 2021. With evolving experiences and perspectives, I felt it necessary to update and refine my message. This book is the third in my latest collection, following my second book, *"I Know It Hurts: Knowing When It Is Time to Let Go."*

Additionally, I have created a supportive community for women navigating their own journeys. Join us on Facebook at [W2W REAL TALK](), where wounded and aspirational women can connect and share their experiences, both collectively and privately.

www.ingramcontent.com/pod-product-compliance
Lightning Source LLC
Chambersburg PA
CBHW070554010526
44118CB00012B/1313